This sakhi book belongs to:

....

This book was devised, designed and completed by volunteers from
Sikh History And Religious Education (S.H.A.R.E.)

Illustrations by Cristian Rodriguez.

Published by Sikh History and Religious Education

Registered Charity Number: 1120428

Khalsa@sharecharityuk.com

S H A R E

Dedicated to all the men and women
saint-soldiers who have fought for humanity...
and continue to.

This is a sakhi about <u>Mata Bhaag Kaur</u> (or Mai Bhago, as she is commonly known). Mata Bhaag Kaur was born in a village in present day <u>Amritsar</u>.

Her <u>ancestors</u> had embraced Sikhi during the times of <u>Guru Arjun Dev Jee</u>, the 5th Guru of the Sikhs.

Her parents had raised her as a strong Sikh woman. She knew all her <u>Paath</u>, was practiced in warfare and the use of arms, and she did seva of all those around her. When she was young, her parents took her to have <u>Darshan</u> of the 9th Guru, Guru Tegh Bahadar Jee.

Her family were <u>initiated</u> into the Khalsa family at the first ever <u>Amrit Sanchaar</u>, in 1699 <u>Anandpur</u> Sahib.

Mata Bhaag Kaur holds a very important place in our <u>heritage</u> and is remembered as a very strong warrior princess. She was married to Nidhan Singh.

The <u>Mughals</u> ruled what is now present day India for a very long time. They wanted everyone in the land to follow their religion.

The <u>Khalsa</u> believes that you should not be forced to be another religion, so from the time of <u>Guru Hargobind Sahib Jee</u>, the 6th Guru, Sikhs had always fought for <u>humanity</u>.

In 1705, the long on-going <u>battle of Chamkaur</u> was taking place. The Khalsa were living in the jungles for months without any water or food. Many soldiers were wounded but they were still strong in spirit.

After sometime, a <u>regiment</u>, led by Bhai Maha Singh, felt they were too weak and not able to fight anymore.

Bhai Maha Singh and his 39 soldiers approached <u>Guru Gobind Singh Jee</u> and asked for permission to leave.

The Guru granted permission to the Soldiers, but asked them to sign a piece of paper that stated that 'He was no longer their Guru and they were no longer His Sikhs'.

When the 40 soldiers returned home, they met Mata Bhaag Kaur. She asked about the Guru. "Has the battle been won?"

The soldiers told Mata Bhaag Kaur they had left the Guru on the battlefield and returned home.

Mata Bhaag Kaur filled with warrior <u>emotion</u>, collected food and weapon supplies and prepared herself for battle.

She was so hurt to learn that her Guru had been left, that she decided to go and stand with the Guru and fight with Him, for humanity.

Realising what they had done, the 40 soldiers also climbed onto they horses and rode off, following Mata Bhaag Kaur.

Mata Bhaag Kaur and the 40 soldiers set up their positions near Khidrana. The enemy approached and a fierce battle broke out.

Mata Bhaag Kaur and the 40 soldiers were out numbered but fought hard and long. They were <u>victorious</u> and the enemy retreated.

Guru Gobind Singh Jee arrived at the battlefield and looked around.

Guru Jee saw a wounded Singh on the ground and recognised it was Bhai Maha Singh, the leader of the 39 soldiers that left Him.

Guru Jee put Bhai Maha Singh's head on His knee and used his <u>kamarkasa</u> to wipe the blood and tears from his eyes.

Guru Jee said, 'Ask whatever you will, the house of Guru Nanak is open to you'.

Bhai Maha Singh said, 'Oh my lord and master. Please forgive us for leaving you. Please destroy the letter we signed and make us your sikhs once more'.

Guru Jee, being all-knowing, had the letter in His <u>kamarkasa</u>. He took the letter out and tore it up.

Mata Bhaag Kaur was hurt in the courageous battle, and Guru Jee ensured her wounds were tended to.

Mata Bhaag Kaur stayed with Guru Jee in His army at Nanded. She was placed as His personal bodyguard.

She was present with Guru Jee when He recruited <u>Baba Banda Singh Bahadar</u>, who later went on to form the <u>Khalsa Raj</u>.

Mata Bhaag Kaur remained with Guru Jee until 1708, when Guru Jee infused the Light of Nanak into <u>Sri Guru Granth Sahib Jee</u>—the eternal Master and <u>Guru</u> of the Sikhs.

Mata Bhaag Kaur was the one who showed the 40 soldiers that leaving Guru Jee was wrong.

Mata Bhaag Kaur shows us that girls can be just as strong as boys, sometime stronger.

Mata Bhaag Kaur teaches us, that love and faith in <u>Guru Jee</u> is the most important thing in the world.

Lets See what you learnt!

1. At the time of which Guru, did Mata Bhaag Kaur's family become Sikhs?

    _____

2. When Mata Bhaag Kaur was young, which Guru did she meet?

    _____

3. How many soldiers did she show, that its wrong to leave the Guru?

    _____

4. What was the name of Mata Bhaag Kaurs husband?

    _____

5. What year was the fierce on-going battle of Chamkaur?

    _____

WELL DONE!

<u>Glossary</u>

Amrit: Ambrosial Nectar (immortal)

Amritsar: historically known as Ramdaspur, city – spiritual centre for the Sikhs

Anadpur Sahib: Holy city of bliss, the first Amrit Sanchaar took place here

Ancestors: Any person whom one is descended from; parent, grandparents etc

Baba Banda Singh Bahadur: Military commander. Avenged the execution of 9th Guru and two younger sons of the 10th Guru. Established Khalsa Raj

Battle of Chamkaur: Ropar district of the Punjab was the scene of two battles

Darshan: Holy sight, vision

Faith: confidence or trust in a person, thing, deity, or in the doctrines or teachings of a religion

Guru (Jee) : Gu - Dark Ru—light (darkness into Light)

Heritage: Something that is received (inherited) from the past

Humanity: Humankind, Human beings collectively

Initiated: Process to become apart of something, society, group, club etc

Khalsa: Pure, someone who has received Amrit

Mata Bhaag Kaur: Strong Sikh woman, who was bodyguard to the 10th Guru

Mughal: Islamic empire, ruled over India since 1526

Nanded: Second largest city in Maharashtra, India. Place where 10th Guru resided after the death of Aurangzeb

Regiment: Military Unit

Retreated: Withdrawal of military forces

Sacrifice: Bloodless or blood offering (in the Name of God)

Sakhi: Real life story

Sanchaar: (Amrit Sanchaar) - Sikh ceremony of initiation or baptism

Seva: Selfless service

Sikh: follower of Sikhism, a monotheistic religion that originated in the 15th century in the Punjab region. The term "Sikh" means disciple, student. A Sikh is a disciple/subject of the Guru.

Spirit: The vital principle or animating force within living beings or Incorporeal consciousness

Victorious: Being the winner in a contest or struggle

Warfare: The waging of war against an enemy; armed conflict